Chief Justice Earl Warren and the People Behind the Constitutional Revolution A Chapter Book

Joseline Jean-Louis Hardrick

CHIEF JUSTICE EARL WARREN AND THE PEOPLE BEHIND THE CONSTITUTIONAL REVOLUTION A CHAPTER BOOK

First edition. June 29, 2026.

ISBN: 978-1958912782

Written by Joseline Hardrick.

Table of Contents

To the future lawyers, judges, and advocates who will work to make the Constitution's promises real.

Chapter 1

The Governor Everyone Wanted

Long before Earl Warren became Chief Justice of the United States, he was one of the most powerful politicians in America.

He wasn't born into wealth or political influence.

He was born in Los Angeles, California, in 1891, to hardworking immigrant parents. His father worked on the railroad, and his family believed in honesty, education, and public service.

Those lessons stayed with Earl throughout his life.

After graduating from law school at the University of California, Berkeley, Warren became a prosecutor in Alameda County.

A prosecutor represents the government in criminal cases. Warren believed that laws should be enforced fairly and that public officials should earn the people's trust.

He worked hard.

People noticed.

Soon he became Alameda County's district attorney.

Then he became California's attorney general.

By 1942, Earl Warren was elected Governor of California.

California was already one of the nation's largest and fastest-growing states.

Leading it was no small job.

Governor Warren gained a reputation for being practical, honest, and willing to work with people from both political parties.

Today we call that bipartisan leadership.

At the time, it made Warren enormously popular.

In fact, during his reelection campaign in 1946, something remarkable happened.

He won both the Republican and Democratic primaries.

Candidates normally belong to one political party.

Warren won support from both.

It was almost unheard of.

His popularity spread far beyond California.

Republican leaders began talking about him as a future president.

Newspapers called him one of the most respected governors in America.

People admired his calm leadership and ability to solve problems.

But Warren's influence reached even farther.

In 1948, Republicans gathered in Philadelphia to choose their presidential nominee.

Several candidates hoped to win the convention.

None had enough delegates.

Earl Warren entered the convention with delegates of his own.

He knew he probably would not become the nominee.

But he understood something important.

The candidate who earned his support might become president.

Political reporters called leaders like Warren "kingmakers."

A kingmaker does not become king.

A kingmaker helps decide who will be like a king.

Although the U.S. Constitution bans kings (and queens), we do have politicians with enormous power and influence. Warren was one of them.

Warren eventually threw his support behind New York Governor Thomas E. Dewey.

Dewey won the Republican nomination.

Although Dewey lost the election to President Harry Truman, Warren's national reputation continued to grow.

Four years later, another presidential election approached.

Again, Republicans searched for a leader.

Again, Earl Warren's name appeared near the top of every list.

Many people believed the popular governor from California might soon become President of the United States.

History, however, had other plans.

The next chapter of Warren's life would begin with a presidential campaign, an unexpected bargain, and a surprising appointment that no one saw coming.

It would take him from the governor's mansion in Sacramento to the highest court in the nation.

Not as an associate justice.

But as Chief Justice of the United States.

Chapter 2

The Unexpected Appointment

By 1952, Earl Warren had become one of the most recognizable politicians in America.

He wanted to be president.

Like several other Republican leaders, he entered the race for the party's nomination.

But there was one problem.

Another candidate had become a national hero.

General Dwight D. Eisenhower.

Americans knew Eisenhower as the Supreme Allied Commander who helped lead the Allies to victory during World War II.

He was admired across the country.

When the Republican National Convention opened in Chicago, it quickly became clear that Eisenhower had the momentum.

Warren still had something valuable.

Delegates.

California had a large number of votes at the convention, and Warren controlled many of them.

Once again, he found himself in the position of kingmaker.

This time, he backed Eisenhower.

According to Warren, Eisenhower privately promised that if a vacancy opened on the United States Supreme Court, Warren would receive the appointment.

Whether every detail of that conversation occurred exactly as Warren later remembered has been debated by historians.

But everyone agrees on what happened next.

Eisenhower won the election.

He became the thirty-fourth President of the United States.

Earl Warren returned to California as governor.

Then, on September 8, 1953, something completely unexpected happened.

Chief Justice Fred Vinson suffered a heart attack.

He died suddenly at the age of sixty-three.

The nation was shocked.

The Supreme Court suddenly had no leader.

President Eisenhower had an important decision to make.

He could appoint anyone who met the constitutional requirements.

Many expected him to choose an experienced federal judge.

Others expected a respected legal scholar.

Instead, Eisenhower chose Earl Warren.

The decision surprised many Americans.

Warren had never served as a judge.

Not on a trial court.

Not on an appeals court.

Not anywhere.

His experience came from public service—as a prosecutor, attorney general, governor, and national political leader.

Some people wondered whether he was qualified.

Others believed his leadership mattered more than judicial experience.

The Constitution does not require Supreme Court justices to have served as judges before joining the Court.

In fact, several justices throughout history had come from politics, government service, or private law practice.

Still, appointing someone directly to the position of **Chief Justice** without prior judicial experience was extraordinary.

On October 5, 1953, Earl Warren took the oath of office.

He did not begin as an associate justice.

He sat immediately in the center chair.

The chair reserved for the Chief Justice of the United States.

No one—not President Eisenhower, not Earl Warren, not the American people—could have known what would happen next.

Over the next sixteen years, Warren would lead one of the most influential Supreme Courts in American history.

The decisions made by the Warren Court would reshape public education, voting rights, criminal justice, free speech, privacy, religious liberty, and civil rights.

The man who had never been a judge was about to become one of the most important judges America had ever known.

His first great test would come only months later.

A little girl named Linda Brown was waiting outside a school she was not allowed to attend.

Chapter 3

Linda Brown's Long Walk

On some mornings, Linda Brown walked past a school she was not allowed to attend.

The building stood only a few blocks from her home in Topeka, Kansas. It was close enough that she could see it. Close enough that she could hear children laughing on the playground.

But Linda could not go there.

Instead, she had to travel much farther to reach the school assigned to Black children.

Linda was only a little girl, but even children know when something feels unfair.

Her father, Oliver Brown, knew it too.

At the time, many states had laws requiring Black and white students to attend separate schools. Supporters of segregation claimed the schools were "separate but equal."

But often they were not equal at all.

Many Black schools had fewer resources, older buildings, worn-out textbooks, and less funding. Even when facilities looked similar, segregation carried a message that hurt deeply: some children mattered more than others.

For decades, this system had been protected by a Supreme Court case called *Plessy v. Ferguson*. Decided in 1896, *Plessy* had allowed segregation under the idea of "separate but equal."

The law said separate was acceptable.

Many Americans knew it was not.

The National Association for the Advancement of Colored People—the NAACP—had spent years challenging segregation. Their lawyers searched for families willing to stand up and tell their stories.

One of those lawyers was a man named Thurgood Marshall.

Marshall was brilliant, determined, and fearless. He traveled across the country fighting laws that treated Black Americans as second-class citizens.

When Oliver Brown agreed to become part of the lawsuit, he joined many other parents from different states who wanted something simple:

Equal treatment for their children.

The lawsuit became known as *Brown v. Board of Education of Topeka.*

Soon similar cases from South Carolina, Virginia, Delaware, and Washington, D.C., were joined together.

The question before the Supreme Court was enormous.

Could segregation in public schools continue?

Or did it violate the Constitution?

The justices listened carefully.

Lawyers presented evidence showing the harm segregation caused. They described unequal schools. They explained how separation affected children's confidence and opportunities.

One important study showed that many Black children, after growing up in segregated schools, had begun to believe the cruel message society was sending them—that they were somehow less valuable.

The justices knew this case was different.

This was not only about school buildings.

It was about dignity.

It was about belonging.

It was about whether the Constitution's promise of equal protection applied to everyone.

Inside the Supreme Court, the justices debated.

Some worried about how the nation would react.

Others wondered how quickly change could happen.

Chief Justice Earl Warren faced a difficult challenge. The Court could issue a divided decision, with some justices agreeing and others disagreeing.

Or the Court could try to speak with one voice.

Warren believed the nation needed unity.

He spent months talking with the other justices, listening to concerns, answering questions, and building agreement.

Finally, on May 17, 1954, the Court announced its decision.

The courtroom fell silent.

Chief Justice Warren read the opinion.

"In the field of public education," he declared, "separate educational facilities are inherently unequal."

Those words changed America.

The Court had unanimously ruled that school segregation violated the Equal Protection Clause of the Fourteenth Amendment.

Plessy v. Ferguson would no longer control public education.

For many families, the decision brought joy.

Parents cried.

Children celebrated.

Civil rights leaders rejoiced.

But not everyone was happy.

Across parts of the country, resistance appeared almost immediately.

Some politicians promised to fight the ruling.

Some school districts delayed integration.

Some communities became angry.

The battle for equality was far from over.

The Supreme Court had opened the door.

Now America would have to decide whether to walk through it.

For Linda Brown, the case became part of history.

For Thurgood Marshall, it became one of the greatest victories of his career.

And for Earl Warren, it became the first landmark decision of a Court that would transform the meaning of the Constitution for generations.

A little girl's long walk to school had helped change the nation.

Sometimes history begins with armies.
Sometimes it begins with presidents.
And sometimes it begins with a child asking a simple question:
"Why can't I go to that school?"

Chapter 4

The Chief Justice

The decision in *Brown v. Board of Education* made headlines across America.

Some people celebrated.

Others were furious.

But inside the Supreme Court, the work continued.

One case could change a nation, but the Warren Court would hear hundreds more.

As the years passed, Earl Warren became known for something unusual.

He knew how to bring people together.

The Supreme Court was made up of nine justices. Each came from a different background. Each had different experiences and ideas about the Constitution.

Some agreed often.

Some disagreed regularly.

Yet Warren had a remarkable talent. He listened carefully. He treated his colleagues with respect. He worked hard to find common ground.

Many of his fellow justices eventually gave him a nickname:

"The Super Chief."

It wasn't because he had special powers.

It wasn't because he was the smartest person in every room.

It was because he could lead.

And leadership mattered.

The Court's decisions carried enormous weight. A divided Court could still make law, but a united Court often carried greater authority.

Warren understood that.

He believed that when possible, the Court should speak with one voice.

One of the people helping shape that voice was Justice William Brennan.

Brennan was brilliant, energetic, and persuasive. Many historians consider him one of the most influential justices in Supreme Court history.

Another was Justice Hugo Black.

Black believed strongly in protecting constitutional rights. He often argued that the words of the Constitution should be followed closely and consistently.

Justice William O. Douglas served longer than any justice in American history. He fiercely defended individual liberty and often challenged government power.

Then there was Justice John Marshall Harlan.

Sometimes called "The Great Dissenter," Harlan did not always agree with the majority. Yet even when he disagreed, his opinions were thoughtful and deeply respected.

The Warren Court was not a team of identical thinkers.

It was a team of strong personalities.

That was what made it work.

The justices argued.

They debated.

They challenged one another.

They rewrote opinions.

Sometimes they changed each other's minds.

And sometimes they did not.

As new justices joined the Court, the conversations grew even richer.

One of the most historic arrivals came in 1967.

His name was Thurgood Marshall.

Years earlier, Marshall had stood before the Court arguing *Brown v. Board of Education*.

Now he would sit on the bench itself.

He became the first Black justice in the history of the United States Supreme Court.

For Marshall, it was an cxtraordinary journey.

He had fought segregation as a lawyer.

He had challenged unfair laws across the country.

Now he would help decide the meaning of the Constitution from the nation's highest court.

Many people saw his appointment as a symbol of progress.

Others saw it as proof that *Brown* had helped change America.

Marshall brought something unique to the Court.

He had spent years representing ordinary people whose rights had been ignored.

He knew what discrimination looked like.

He knew what injustice felt like.

And he carried those experiences with him into every case.

The justices often disagreed about outcomes.

But they shared one responsibility.

They had sworn to uphold the Constitution.

Together they faced difficult questions.

Could police search someone's home without a warrant?

Should poor defendants receive lawyers?

Do students have free speech rights?

Can government tell people who they may marry?

Can states draw voting districts unfairly?

Can officials punish newspapers for criticizing them?

Again and again, these questions landed on the justices' desks.

Again and again, they had to decide.

The answers would affect millions of people they would never meet.

Children.

Teachers.

Parents.

Journalists.

Voters.

Workers.

Prisoners.

Students.

The Constitution belonged to all of them.

As the Warren Court continued its work, one thing became clear.

The Court was not simply interpreting old words.

It was deciding how those words would live in the modern world.

And some of the most important decisions were still ahead.

Soon another ordinary person would step forward.

Her name was Dollree Mapp.

And a dispute that began in her own home would change police practices across America.

Chapter 5

Dollree Mapp Says No

On a warm day in Cleveland, Ohio, police officers arrived at a house looking for someone.

They believed a suspect might be hiding inside.

The house belonged to a woman named Dollree Mapp.

The officers knocked on the door.

Dollree Mapp answered.

The police wanted to come in and search the house.

Mapp wanted to see a warrant.

A warrant is a legal document signed by a judge. It gives police permission to search a specific place for specific evidence.

The Fourth Amendment to the Constitution protects people from unreasonable searches and seizures. The amendment exists because the Founders remembered a time when government officials could enter homes with little justification.

The Constitution drew a line.

Government power was not supposed to be unlimited.

So when the officers asked to enter, Mapp stood her ground.

"Show me a warrant," she demanded.

The officers left.

But later they returned.

This time they forced their way into the house.

Mapp again demanded to see a warrant.

An officer held up a piece of paper.

Before she could examine it, the police took it away.

Years later, questions would remain about whether a valid warrant had ever existed at all.

The officers searched everywhere.

They opened drawers.

They searched closets.

They looked through rooms from top to bottom.

They never found the suspect they were seeking.

Instead, they found materials they claimed violated Ohio law.

Mapp was arrested.

Soon she found herself facing criminal charges.

Her lawyers argued that the evidence should never have been used.

Why?

Because if the search itself was illegal, shouldn't the evidence be illegal too?

The question was bigger than Dollree Mapp.

Imagine a referee who lets one team break every rule but still counts the points.

Would that be fair?

Many people thought the same principle should apply to police searches.

If officers violate the Constitution to gather evidence, should courts reward that behavior?

The case eventually reached the United States Supreme Court.

By then, Earl Warren and the other justices had already decided important civil rights cases.

Now they faced another difficult question.

How should courts protect the Fourth Amendment?

The justices listened carefully.

Some argued that excluding illegally obtained evidence was necessary.

Otherwise, what would stop police from ignoring constitutional limits?

Others worried that guilty people might go free.

The issue was not simple.

Protecting liberty often requires difficult choices.

When the Court announced its decision in 1961, it sided with Mapp.

The Warren Court ruled that evidence obtained through unconstitutional searches generally could not be used in state criminal trials.

The rule became known as the exclusionary rule.

The idea was straightforward.

The government should not benefit from violating constitutional rights.

Justice Tom Clark wrote the majority opinion.

The decision dramatically changed police practices across the country.

Officers became more careful about obtaining warrants.

Judges became more involved in reviewing searches.

Lawyers paid closer attention to how evidence was collected.

The ruling did not mean police could never search homes.

It did not mean criminals could never be convicted.

It meant that the Constitution's protections had consequences.

Rights written on paper had to mean something in real life.

For Dollree Mapp, the decision was a victory.

For the Warren Court, it was another step in defining what constitutional liberty looked like.

And for millions of Americans, it reinforced an important lesson:

The government has power.

But that power has limits.

The Fourth Amendment exists to make sure those limits are respected.

The next case would ask a different question.

What happens when someone is accused of a crime but cannot afford a lawyer?

The answer would come from a prison cell in Florida, where a man named Clarence Gideon sat down with a pencil and a piece of paper.

And with those simple tools, he began changing American history.

Chapter 6

The Prisoner Who Wrote the Supreme Court

Clarence Earl Gideon was not a famous man.

He was not wealthy.

He was not a politician.

He was not a lawyer.

Yet his name would eventually appear in one of the most important Supreme Court cases in American history.

It all began in a small pool hall in Panama City, Florida.

One morning, someone reported that the pool hall had been broken into. Cigarettes, beer, and money were missing.

Police investigated.

Soon they arrested Clarence Gideon and charged him with burglary.

When Gideon appeared in court, he knew he needed a lawyer.

The government had prosecutors.

The prosecutor understood the law.

The prosecutor knew how trials worked.

Gideon did not.

So he asked the judge for a lawyer.

The judge shook his head.

Florida law only provided free lawyers in certain serious cases, usually those involving the death penalty.

Gideon was on his own.

Standing in court, he tried to defend himself.

He questioned witnesses.

He made arguments.

He did the best he could.

But he had no legal training.

The prosecutor did.

The jury found Gideon guilty.

He was sentenced to five years in prison.

For many people, that might have been the end of the story.

For Gideon, it was only the beginning.

Sitting in prison, he thought about what had happened.

The Sixth Amendment says that people accused of crimes have the right to the assistance of counsel.

Counsel is another word for a lawyer.

But if a person is too poor to hire a lawyer, what good is that right?

The question would not leave him alone.

One day Gideon picked up a pencil.

He found some paper.

Then he began to write.

His petition was not fancy.

It was not filled with complicated legal language.

It was handwritten.

Simple.

Direct.

But it asked a powerful question.

Had his constitutional rights been violated?

The letter traveled all the way to Washington, D.C.

Eventually it landed at the United States Supreme Court.

Thousands of requests reach the Court every year.

Most are denied.

This one was different.

The justices agreed to hear Gideon's case.

Soon lawyers were appointed to represent him before the Court.

One of them was Abe Fortas, a highly respected attorney who would later become a Supreme Court justice himself.

Fortas argued that a fair trial is impossible when one side has a trained lawyer and the other side has none.

The Constitution promised more than a courtroom.

It promised justice.

The Warren Court listened carefully.

The justices knew the decision could affect courts across the nation.

If Gideon was right, states would have to provide lawyers to many criminal defendants who could not afford one.

That would change the justice system forever.

In 1963, the Court announced its decision.

The ruling was unanimous.

Every justice agreed.

The Court declared that the right to counsel is fundamental.

If a person faces serious criminal charges and cannot afford a lawyer, the state must provide one.

Justice Hugo Black wrote the opinion.

He explained that lawyers are not luxuries.

They are necessities.

Without legal representation, many defendants would have little chance of receiving a fair trial.

The decision transformed American courts.

Across the country, states created and expanded public defender offices.

Thousands of people who previously would have stood alone now had lawyers to represent them.

But the story was not over.

After the Supreme Court ruled in his favor, Gideon received a new trial.

This time he had a lawyer.

The lawyer challenged the evidence.

The lawyer questioned witnesses.

The lawyer did what lawyers are trained to do.

When the trial ended, the jury found Clarence Gideon not guilty.

The man who had written a petition from prison walked free.

His case became known as *Gideon v. Wainwright*.

Today, law students study it.

Lawyers cite it.

Judges rely on it.

But its lesson is simple enough for anyone to understand:

Justice works best when everyone has a voice.

And sometimes the person who changes history is not a president, a governor, or a judge.

Sometimes it is a prisoner with a pencil.

The Warren Court had protected another constitutional right.

Soon it would face another question.

What if a person does not even know they have rights?

The answer would come from Arizona, where a man named Ernesto Miranda sat in a police station answering questions he did not realize he could refuse to answer.

Chapter 7

You Have the Right to Remain Silent

In March 1963, a young woman in Phoenix, Arizona, reported a terrible crime.

Police began searching for a suspect.

Soon they arrested a twenty-three-year-old man named Ernesto Miranda.

The officers took Miranda to a police station for questioning.

For two hours they asked him questions.

No lawyer sat beside him.

No judge was present.

No one explained that he could refuse to answer.

No one told him he could ask for an attorney.

Eventually, Miranda signed a written confession.

The paper would become one of the most famous documents in American legal history.

At Miranda's trial, prosecutors introduced the confession as evidence.

The confession helped secure his conviction.

Miranda was sentenced to prison.

To many people, the case seemed finished.

But Miranda's lawyers believed something important had gone wrong.

They focused on two constitutional amendments.

The Fifth Amendment protects people from being forced to testify against themselves.

The Sixth Amendment guarantees the right to a lawyer.

The lawyers asked a simple question:

How can people exercise those rights if they do not know they have them?

The question reached the Supreme Court.

By now, the Warren Court had already decided major cases involving schools, voting, and criminal defendants.

Now the justices faced another challenge.

What protections should exist during police interrogations?

The arguments were intense.

Some people worried that requiring additional warnings would make law enforcement more difficult.

Others argued that constitutional rights mean very little if people are unaware of them.

Inside the Supreme Court, the justices debated.

Could a confession truly be voluntary if a suspect did not understand their rights?

How could courts be sure people knew they had choices?

The decision would affect police departments throughout America.

In 1966, Chief Justice Earl Warren delivered the Court's opinion.

The Court ruled that police must inform suspects of certain constitutional rights before conducting custodial interrogations.

The warnings had to be clear.

People needed to know they had the right to remain silent.

They needed to know that anything they said could be used against them in court.

They needed to know they had the right to consult with a lawyer.

And if they could not afford a lawyer, one could be appointed.

These protections became known as the Miranda warnings.

Today, many people recognize them from television shows and movies.

"You have the right to remain silent."

The words have become part of American culture.

But behind those famous words lies an important constitutional principle.

Rights only matter if people know they exist.

The Court was not saying suspects could never be questioned.

It was not saying police could never solve crimes.

It was saying that constitutional protections must be explained before someone decides whether to speak.

The decision sparked debate across the nation.

Some praised it.

Some criticized it.

Many argued about whether the Court had gone too far.

Yet the ruling endured.

Decades later, Miranda warnings remain one of the most recognizable symbols of constitutional rights.

As for Ernesto Miranda himself, his story had an unexpected twist.

After the Supreme Court's decision, he received a new trial.

This time prosecutors relied on evidence other than the original confession.

Miranda was convicted again.

The case was never really about whether he was guilty.

It was about how government must treat people when exercising its power.

The Warren Court believed the Constitution required rules that protected everyone.

Not just the innocent.

Not just the popular.

Everyone.

Because constitutional rights are tested most when the government believes it has a strong case.

The question is not whether rights are convenient.

The question is whether they are guaranteed.

The Court had answered that question.

But another challenge was waiting.

This one would involve freedom of speech, civil rights protests, newspaper advertisements, and a public official who believed his reputation had been damaged.

The case was called *New York Times v. Sullivan*.

And it would help define how free a free press must be.

Chapter 8

The Advertisement That Changed Free Speech

In the spring of 1960, America was changing.

Across the South, students sat at lunch counters where they were told they could not sit.

Church leaders organized marches.

Families risked their jobs, their homes, and even their lives to demand equal rights.

The Civil Rights Movement was growing stronger every day.

But movements need support.

They need money.

They need attention.

And they need people willing to tell the truth about what is happening.

That is where a newspaper advertisement entered the story.

On March 29, 1960, readers of *The New York Times* opened their newspapers and saw a full-page advertisement titled:

"Heed Their Rising Voices."

The ad asked Americans to support the struggle for civil rights.

It described events happening in the South and called attention to the treatment of civil rights protesters.

The advertisement raised money for the legal defense of Dr. Martin Luther King Jr.

Many people read it and moved on with their day.

But one person paid very close attention.

His name was L. B. Sullivan.

Sullivan was one of the commissioners who supervised the Montgomery, Alabama police department.

Although the advertisement never mentioned him by name, Sullivan believed some of the statements reflected poorly on him and the city government.

He also claimed that parts of the advertisement contained factual mistakes.

The mistakes were relatively minor.

For example, some details about student demonstrations were not perfectly accurate.

But Sullivan believed the errors damaged his reputation.

So he filed a lawsuit.

He sued *The New York Times* for libel.

Libel is a false written statement that harms someone's reputation.

Soon a jury in Alabama ruled in Sullivan's favor.

The jury awarded him $500,000.

At the time, that was an enormous amount of money.

The decision sent shockwaves through the press.

Journalists worried.

Newspapers worried.

Civil rights leaders worried.

If public officials could win huge lawsuits whenever a newspaper made a mistake, what would happen?

Would reporters become afraid to criticize government leaders?

Would newspapers stop publishing controversial stories?

Would people be too frightened to speak out?

The case soon reached the United States Supreme Court.

The justices understood that the stakes were enormous.

The First Amendment protects freedom of speech and freedom of the press.

But freedom of the press does not mean newspapers can knowingly publish lies.

The challenge was finding the right balance.

How much protection should the Constitution provide?

Inside the Court, the justices considered the history of democracy itself.

A free society depends on debate.

People must be able to criticize leaders.

They must be able to question government decisions.

They must be able to discuss public issues openly.

Sometimes those discussions are messy.

Sometimes mistakes happen.

Should every mistake lead to punishment?

In 1964, the Warren Court answered.

The decision was unanimous.

The Court ruled in favor of *The New York Times*.

Justice William Brennan wrote the opinion.

He explained that debate on public issues should be "uninhibited, robust, and wide-open."

The Court created a new rule.

Public officials could not win a libel lawsuit simply because a statement was wrong.

Instead, they had to prove something much more difficult.

They had to prove **actual malice**.

Actual malice does not mean ordinary anger or dislike.

It means that a statement was published knowing it was false or with reckless disregard for whether it was true or false.

That standard changed American law forever.

The ruling gave journalists greater protection when reporting on public officials.

It also gave citizens greater freedom to criticize those in power.

The Court recognized that democracy requires room for mistakes.

Otherwise, fear could silence important conversations.

For civil rights activists, the decision was especially significant.

Newspapers could continue reporting on discrimination and injustice without constantly fearing ruinous lawsuits.

For journalists, it became one of the most important First Amendment cases ever decided.

And for the Warren Court, it was another example of a larger idea.

The Constitution protects more than popular speech.

It protects speech people disagree with.

It protects criticism.

It protects debate.

Because democracy depends on citizens being able to question power.

The case became known as *New York Times v. Sullivan.*

More than sixty years later, its influence remains everywhere.

Every time a newspaper investigates a public official.

Every time a journalist asks a difficult question.

Every time citizens criticize those who govern them.

The legacy of *New York Times v. Sullivan* lives on.

But another important question was waiting for the Court.

This one involved the rights of Native nations and the meaning of sovereignty.

It began on Navajo land, where a dispute over a trading post would become one of the most important tribal sovereignty cases in American history.

The case was called *Williams v. Lee.*

Chapter 9

A Question of Sovereignty

The deserts of the American Southwest stretch for miles.

Red cliffs rise above the horizon.

Dust swirls across open land.

And within that vast landscape lies the Navajo Nation, one of the largest Native nations in the United States.

For generations, the Navajo people governed themselves, maintained their traditions, and operated their own courts.

Yet questions about Native sovereignty often created conflict.

What exactly did sovereignty mean?

Could Native nations govern themselves?

Or could states control what happened on reservation land?

Those questions reached the Supreme Court through a dispute that seemed small at first.

But like many important cases, the issue was much bigger than it appeared.

The case involved a man named Hugh Lee.

Lee owned and operated a trading post on the Navajo Reservation in Arizona.

Trading posts were important places in reservation communities.

Families bought supplies there.

They purchased food, tools, clothing, and household goods.

Many transactions happened on credit.

Customers would buy items and pay later.

One day, a disagreement arose.

Lee claimed that Paul and Marena Williams, members of the Navajo Nation, owed money for goods purchased on credit.

He wanted to collect the debt.

Today that might sound like an ordinary business dispute.

But Lee's next step created a constitutional question.

Instead of filing his lawsuit in a Navajo tribal court, Lee filed it in an Arizona state court.

The Williams family objected.

They argued that the dispute belonged in tribal court.

After all, the events occurred on reservation land.

The Williamses were Navajo citizens.

Why should an outside state court decide the matter?

The disagreement quickly became about much more than money.

It became about self-government.

For centuries, Native nations had fought to preserve their authority.

Treaties had been signed.

Promises had been made.

Yet states and the federal government often challenged tribal power.

Many Native communities worried that allowing state courts to decide reservation disputes would weaken tribal governments.

If tribal courts could not decide cases involving their own citizens on their own land, what power would they have left?

The case eventually reached the United States Supreme Court.

The justices faced a difficult question.

Could Arizona exercise authority over this dispute?

Or would doing so interfere with Navajo self-government?

The Warren Court carefully considered the issue.

The justices examined treaties, history, and the relationship between tribal nations and the United States.

They recognized that Native nations were not simply neighborhoods inside a state.

They were governments.

Governments with their own traditions, laws, and courts.

In 1959, the Court announced its decision.

Justice Hugo Black wrote the opinion.

The Court ruled in favor of the Williams family.

Arizona could not exercise jurisdiction over the dispute.

The case belonged in tribal court.

The Court explained that allowing state courts to take control would undermine tribal authority.

It would interfere with the right of Native nations to govern their own affairs.

The decision became known as *Williams v. Lee.*

For Native communities across the country, the ruling was enormously important.

It strengthened tribal courts.

It affirmed tribal sovereignty.

And it recognized that Native nations possess authority over matters occurring within their own communities.

The case did not solve every issue involving tribal sovereignty.

Many questions would remain.

Some still exist today.

But *Williams v. Lee* became a major step toward recognizing tribal self-government.

For the Warren Court, the decision reflected another important principle.

The Constitution and the law do not belong only to the powerful.

They also protect communities whose voices have often been overlooked.

The Court had protected free speech.

It had protected equal education.

It had protected the right to counsel.

Now it had reinforced the authority of Native nations to govern themselves.

Yet another challenge was approaching.

This one involved a man standing in a police lineup.

Witnesses pointed.

A criminal case moved forward.

But a question lingered:

What happens when a person's future may depend on being identified correctly?

The answer would come in a case called *United States v. Wade*.

And it would shape how fairness works long before a trial even begins.

Chapter 10

The Man in the Lineup

Imagine standing in a line with several strangers.

Bright lights shine overhead.

People stare at your face.

Somebody points.

And that single moment could determine the rest of your life.

That was the concern at the heart of *United States v. Wade.*

The case began after a bank robbery in Texas.

Witnesses described the robber.

Police searched for a suspect.

Eventually they arrested a man named Billy Joe Wade.

After his arrest, officers organized a lineup.

A lineup is a procedure where several people stand together while witnesses attempt to identify the person they believe committed a crime.

The idea sounds simple.

But mistakes happen.

People do not always remember faces perfectly.

Memories can fade.

Stress can affect what witnesses see and recall.

Sometimes a witness honestly believes they identified the right person and still turns out to be mistaken.

That possibility worried Wade's lawyers.

When police conducted the lineup, Wade's attorney was not present.

No lawyer stood beside him.

No lawyer observed the procedure.

No lawyer could challenge anything that seemed unfair.

Yet witnesses later identified Wade as the robber.

Those identifications became important evidence.

At trial, the witnesses again pointed to Wade.

The jury convicted him.

But Wade's lawyers believed something important had gone wrong.

The Sixth Amendment guarantees the right to counsel.

Everyone understood that defendants have lawyers during trials.

But what about events before trial?

What about moments that could dramatically affect the outcome of a case?

Could a lineup be one of those moments?

The question reached the Warren Court.

The justices understood the danger.

A mistaken identification can be powerful evidence.

Jurors often trust eyewitnesses.

After all, if someone says, "I saw him do it," that sounds convincing.

But history had shown that eyewitnesses can sometimes be wrong.

And once a witness identifies a suspect, that identification can influence everything that follows.

The justices asked themselves:

Should a defendant have a lawyer present during a lineup?

Would that help ensure fairness?

Or would it place too many burdens on law enforcement?

The arguments were intense.

Lawyers for Wade argued that lineups are critical stages of a criminal prosecution.

What happens there can shape the entire case.

Without legal representation, defendants might be unable to challenge unfair procedures.

The government argued that requiring lawyers at lineups would make investigations more difficult.

The Court had to balance efficiency and fairness.

As it had done many times before, the Warren Court focused on constitutional protections.

In 1967, the Court announced its decision.

The justices ruled that post-indictment lineups are a critical stage of the criminal process.

Because of that, defendants generally have a right to have counsel present.

Justice William Brennan wrote the majority opinion.

The Court recognized that mistaken identifications can have serious consequences.

A lawyer's presence helps protect the fairness of the process.

The ruling did not guarantee that witnesses would always be correct.

It did not prevent police from conducting lineups.

Instead, it created additional safeguards.

The goal was simple:

Make sure justice is based on fairness rather than chance.

The decision became known as *United States v. Wade*.

Today, the case remains an important part of criminal procedure.

Law students study it.

Judges cite it.

Lawyers rely on it when challenging identification procedures.

For the Warren Court, the case reflected a familiar theme.

Constitutional rights do not begin only when a trial starts.

Sometimes rights matter most before a jury ever enters the courtroom.

The Court continued building a justice system that sought not only convictions but fairness.

Because finding the truth requires more than pointing a finger.

It requires procedures people can trust.

And soon the Court would confront another question about fairness.

This time, the issue would involve voting.

Millions of Americans could cast ballots.

But not all votes carried the same weight.

The Constitution promised representation.

The question was whether every citizen truly received it.

The case was called *Baker v. Carr*.
And it would transform American democracy.

Chapter 11

One Person, One Vote

Most Americans assume that every vote counts equally.

If two people vote in the same election, each person's vote should have the same weight.

At least, that seems fair.

But during the middle of the twentieth century, that was not always true.

In some states, voting districts had not been updated for decades.

Cities grew.

Suburbs expanded.

Populations changed dramatically.

Yet many state legislatures continued using old district maps.

As a result, some districts had far more people than others.

Imagine two classrooms electing a class president.

One classroom has twenty students.

The other has two hundred.

But each classroom gets exactly one vote.

Would that seem fair?

Probably not.

Yet something similar was happening in parts of the United States.

People living in heavily populated cities often had less political power than people living in sparsely populated rural areas.

Their votes counted for less.

Their voices carried less weight.

And many citizens were frustrated.

One of those citizens was Charles Baker.

Baker lived in Tennessee.

For years, Tennessee's legislature had failed to redraw its voting districts even though the state's population had changed dramatically.

Rural districts still enjoyed enormous influence.

Urban voters often found themselves underrepresented.

Baker believed that was unfair.

He and other voters filed a lawsuit.

They argued that Tennessee's voting system violated the Constitution.

The case eventually became known as *Baker v. Carr*.

At first glance, the issue sounded political.

And that created a problem.

For many years, federal courts had often refused to decide disputes involving legislative district maps.

Judges frequently considered those questions "political questions" better left to elected officials.

But what if those elected officials benefited from the unfair system?

What if they had little reason to change it?

That was exactly the problem Baker and the other voters described.

The case reached the Warren Court in 1962.

The justices faced an important question:

Could federal courts hear challenges to unfair voting districts?

Or were those issues completely beyond judicial review?

The decision would affect elections across America.

The Court listened carefully.

The lawyers for Baker argued that unequal districts denied citizens equal protection under the Fourteenth Amendment.

If some votes counted more than others, was that really equal representation?

The lawyers for Tennessee argued that courts should stay out of the matter.

District maps, they claimed, were political questions.

The Warren Court disagreed.

Justice William Brennan wrote the majority opinion.

The Court ruled that federal courts could hear cases challenging legislative districting systems.

That may sound like a technical legal decision.

But its impact was enormous.

For the first time, federal courts had a clear path to review claims of unequal representation.

Suddenly, voters across the nation could challenge unfair district maps.

The ruling opened courthouse doors.

And once those doors opened, many more cases followed.

One of those cases would become even more famous.

It was called *Reynolds v. Sims*.

In that case, the Court would take the next step and announce a principle that Americans still recognize today:

"One person, one vote."

But *Baker v. Carr* came first.

It made that future possible.

The decision transformed democracy.

State legislatures across the country began redrawing districts.

Maps changed.

Representation changed.

Political power shifted.

Millions of citizens gained a stronger voice in government.

For the Warren Court, the case reflected another core belief.

Democracy works best when every citizen matters.

Not just some citizens.

Not just the powerful.

Everyone.

The Constitution's promise of equality could not stop at the courtroom door.

It had to reach the voting booth too.

And the Court was not finished yet.

Soon another case would ask an even bigger question:

If every vote should count equally, how should states draw their legislative districts?

The answer would come in *Reynolds v. Sims*.

And it would give America one of its most famous constitutional principles.

Chapter 12

One Person, One Vote Revisited

Two years after *Baker v. Carr*, the Supreme Court faced another voting rights challenge.

This time, the case came from Alabama.

And this time, the Court would go even further.

Like Tennessee, Alabama had not updated many of its legislative districts for years.

The state's population had changed dramatically.

Cities had grown.

Towns had expanded.

But the voting maps remained frozen in the past.

As a result, some districts contained many more people than others.

Yet each district elected the same number of representatives.

That meant some citizens had far greater political influence than others.

Imagine two school councils.

One represents one hundred students.

The other represents ten thousand.

Yet both councils get exactly one seat.

Most people would immediately recognize the problem.

The students in the larger group would have far less influence.

That was exactly what many Alabama voters believed was happening.

One of those voters was M. O. Sims.

Sims and other citizens challenged Alabama's district maps.

They argued that the system violated the Equal Protection Clause of the Fourteenth Amendment.

The case became known as *Reynolds v. Sims.*

When the dispute reached the Warren Court, the justices understood the stakes.

The case was not simply about Alabama.

States across the nation were watching.

If the Court ruled for Sims, legislatures throughout America might have to redraw their districts.

The question was simple to ask but difficult to answer:

Should every citizen's vote carry roughly the same weight?

The justices considered the Constitution carefully.

They examined the purpose of representative government.

They looked at what democracy requires.

And they thought about what equality means in practice.

Chief Justice Earl Warren wrote the Court's opinion.

His answer was clear.

In a democracy, legislators represent people.

Not acres.

Not counties.

Not empty stretches of land.

People.

If representatives serve people, then districts should be based on population.

Otherwise, some citizens receive more political power than others.

The Court ruled that legislative districts must be apportioned so that citizens are represented as equally as possible.

From this decision came one of the most famous phrases in constitutional law:

"One person, one vote."

The words became a powerful symbol of democratic equality.

Every citizen's voice mattered.

Every citizen's vote mattered.

No person's ballot should count more simply because of where they lived.

The ruling transformed American politics.

States across the country began redrawing their legislative maps.

Old systems were challenged.

District boundaries changed.

Political power shifted.

Many growing cities gained greater representation.

Millions of voters gained a stronger voice in government.

Not everyone welcomed the decision.

Some politicians resisted.

Some communities complained.

Others feared losing influence they had held for decades.

But the Warren Court believed that democracy required fairness.

The Constitution's promise of equal protection could not mean one thing in theory and another in practice.

Equality had to be real.

For Earl Warren, the decision reflected a larger principle.

Government belongs to the people.

All the people.

Not just a favored few.

The ruling became one of the most significant voting rights decisions in Supreme Court history.

Even today, courts continue to debate questions about voting districts and representation.

But *Reynolds v. Sims* established a foundation that still shapes elections throughout the United States.

The Warren Court had now changed public education, criminal justice, free speech, tribal sovereignty, and voting rights.

Yet another constitutional question was waiting.

This one involved marriage.

A husband and wife had crossed a state line.

Their love was legal in one place.

A crime in another.

The case would become one of the most famous civil rights decisions ever issued.

Their names were Richard and Mildred Loving.

And their fight would ask a simple but powerful question:

Can the government decide who you are allowed to marry?

Chapter 13

The Lovings Return Home

Richard Loving fell in love with Mildred Jeter long before their names appeared in history books.

They grew up in Caroline County, Virginia.

They knew the same roads.

The same neighbors.

The same community.

And over time, they fell in love.

To them, their relationship seemed simple.

They wanted to build a life together.

But Virginia law saw things differently.

Richard was white.

Mildred was Black and Native American.

At the time, Virginia had a law banning interracial marriage.

The law made it a crime for people of different races to marry.

Today, many people find that difficult to imagine.

But in the 1950s, such laws still existed in several states.

Richard and Mildred refused to let the law decide their future.

In 1958, they traveled to Washington, D.C., where interracial marriage was legal.

There, they were married.

Then they returned home to Virginia.

For a short time, everything seemed fine.

Then, one night, police officers entered their home.

The Lovings were asleep in bed.

The officers demanded to know why they were together.

Richard pointed to their marriage certificate hanging on the wall.

It did not matter.

The certificate was valid in Washington, D.C.

Virginia refused to recognize it.

The couple was arrested.

Soon they stood before a judge.

The judge found them guilty.

Then he offered them a choice.

They could go to prison.

Or they could leave Virginia.

The Lovings chose exile.

For twenty-five years.

Imagine being told you could not live in your hometown because of who you married.

Imagine being separated from family, friends, and the place you called home.

That was the reality Richard and Mildred faced.

They moved to Washington, D.C.

But they missed Virginia.

They missed their families.

They wanted their children to grow up where they had grown up.

Most of all, they wanted to live as a married couple without being treated as criminals.

Years later, Mildred decided to seek help.

She wrote a letter to Attorney General Robert F. Kennedy.

That letter eventually led the Lovings to lawyers from the American Civil Liberties Union.

The lawyers agreed to help.

They challenged Virginia's law.

The case slowly made its way through the courts.

Eventually, it reached the United States Supreme Court.

The question before the Warren Court was straightforward:

Could a state prohibit two adults from marrying simply because of their race?

Virginia argued that its law treated everyone equally.

After all, the state punished both people in an interracial marriage.

But the Lovings' lawyers argued that the law was built entirely on racial discrimination.

The Constitution promised equal protection.

How could such a law be equal?

The justices considered the issue carefully.

The answer they reached was unanimous.

In 1967, Chief Justice Earl Warren delivered the Court's opinion.

The Court struck down Virginia's law.

And with it, similar laws across the country.

Warren wrote words that would echo through history:

"The freedom to marry has long been recognized as one of the vital personal rights essential to the orderly pursuit of happiness."

The Court ruled that marriage is a fundamental right.

States could not deny that right based on race.

The decision transformed millions of lives.

Couples who had been forced apart could marry.

Families no longer had to fear criminal prosecution because of race.

The Constitution's promise of equality became more real for countless Americans.

For Richard and Mildred Loving, the victory was deeply personal.

They had never set out to become famous.

They had never asked to become symbols.

They simply wanted what many people want:

The freedom to marry the person they loved.

The Warren Court agreed.

The Constitution protects individuals.

It protects liberty.

And it protects equality.

The Lovings' story became one of the most powerful civil rights victories in American history.

Yet even as the Court defended equality, another challenge was arriving.

This one involved students.

Not adults.

Not politicians.

Not lawyers.

Students.

A group of young people wanted to make a statement about war.

They wore simple black armbands.

Their protest was silent.

But the constitutional question it raised would speak loudly for generations.

The case was called *Tinker v. Des Moines*.

Chapter 14

The Students Who Wore Black Armbands

In 1965, the Vietnam War was growing larger.

More American soldiers were being sent overseas.

Newspaper headlines carried stories of battles and casualties.

Families worried.

Communities argued.

The nation seemed divided.

Even children noticed.

Among them was a thirteen-year-old girl named Mary Beth Tinker.

Mary Beth lived in Iowa with her family.

Like many Americans, the Tinkers talked about the war around the dinner table.

They discussed peace.

They discussed justice.

And they wondered what ordinary people could do to make their voices heard.

As Christmas approached, a group of students decided on a simple protest.

They would wear black armbands to school.

The armbands would honor those who had died in the war and express support for peace.

The protest would be silent.

No shouting.

No signs.

No speeches.

Just black cloth worn around their arms.

The students believed they had a right to express their views.

School officials disagreed.

When administrators learned about the plan, they quickly adopted a rule.

Any student wearing an armband would be asked to remove it.

If the student refused, they would be suspended.

Mary Beth knew the consequences.

So did her brother, John.

And so did their friend Christopher Eckhardt.

Yet they wore the armbands anyway.

When school officials saw them, they demanded that the students remove them.

The students refused.

As promised, the schools suspended them.

The students stayed home until after the protest ended.

For many people, the matter might have ended there.

But the Tinkers believed something important was at stake.

The First Amendment protects freedom of speech.

Did that protection apply only to adults?

Or did students have constitutional rights too?

The students and their families filed a lawsuit.

The case slowly moved through the courts.

Eventually, it reached the Supreme Court.

The justices faced a question that had never been answered so clearly before:

Do students have free speech rights at school?

Some people argued that schools needed order and discipline.

Teachers could not run classrooms if every student ignored the rules.

Others argued that schools exist to teach citizenship.

How could students learn democracy if they were not allowed to express their opinions?

The Warren Court listened carefully.

The justices examined the facts.

The students had not disrupted classes.

They had not threatened anyone.

They had not caused violence.

They had simply worn black armbands.

In 1969, the Court announced its decision.

Justice Abe Fortas wrote the majority opinion.

The students won.

The Court declared that students do not lose their constitutional rights simply because they enter a school building.

Fortas wrote one of the most famous sentences in Supreme Court history:

Students do not "shed their constitutional rights to freedom of speech or expression at the schoolhouse gate."

The Court explained that schools may limit speech that substantially disrupts education.

But peaceful expression is different.

The Constitution protects unpopular ideas.

It protects minority opinions.

And it protects the right to disagree.

The decision became known as *Tinker v. Des Moines Independent Community School District*.

Today, students across America still learn about the case.

Its influence reaches classrooms, student newspapers, assemblies, and school clubs.

The ruling reminds us that young people are citizens too.

Their voices matter.

Their ideas matter.

Their rights matter.

For the Warren Court, *Tinker* reflected a principle that appeared again and again throughout its decisions.

The Constitution belongs to everyone.

Not just judges.

Not just politicians.

Not just adults.

Everyone.

Even students wearing black armbands.

As the Warren era approached its final years, another constitutional question was waiting.

This one involved privacy.

Not in a home.

Not in a school.

But inside a small public phone booth.

A man named Charles Katz believed his conversation was private.

The government disagreed.

The case would help define privacy in the modern age.

And it would ask a question that remains important today:

When technology changes, do constitutional rights change too?

The case was called *Katz v. United States*.

Chapter 15

The Phone Booth

Today, people carry phones in their pockets.

They text.

They call.

They send messages across the world in seconds.

But in the 1960s, things were different.

If you needed to make a private phone call while away from home, you often stepped into a phone booth.

The booth was small.

It had glass walls.

A telephone hung inside.

When the door closed, it created a little space between you and the busy world outside.

That little space would become the center of a constitutional revolution.

The story began with a man named Charles Katz.

Katz often used a public phone booth in Los Angeles.

Federal agents suspected that he was involved in illegal gambling activities.

They wanted to know what he was saying during his phone calls.

But there was a problem.

The agents did not have a warrant.

Instead, they attached a listening device to the outside of the phone booth.

The device recorded Katz's conversations.

The agents listened.

The recordings became evidence.

Soon Katz was arrested and charged.

At trial, prosecutors used the recordings against him.

Katz's lawyers objected.

They argued that the government had violated the Fourth Amendment.

The Fourth Amendment protects people from unreasonable searches and seizures.

But the government had an answer.

The agents had never entered the phone booth.

They had not broken down a door.

They had not searched Katz's home.

The listening device was attached to the outside of the booth.

The government argued that no search had occurred.

The case eventually reached the Supreme Court.

The justices faced a new challenge.

Technology was changing.

The Constitution had been written long before telephones existed.

How should constitutional protections apply in a modern world?

The question was bigger than a phone booth.

It was really about privacy.

When should people expect their conversations to remain private?

Could the government listen whenever it wanted?

Or did constitutional protections follow people wherever they went?

The Warren Court considered these questions carefully.

The justices understood that technology would continue to evolve.

The Constitution had to remain relevant.

In 1967, the Court announced its decision.

The justices ruled in favor of Katz.

Justice Potter Stewart wrote the majority opinion.

He explained that the Fourth Amendment protects people, not places.

Those words changed constitutional law forever.

Before *Katz*, courts often focused on physical spaces.

Had police entered a house?

Had they trespassed on property?

Had they physically searched something?

After *Katz*, the focus shifted.

The Court began asking whether a person had a reasonable expectation of privacy.

Charles Katz entered the phone booth.

He closed the door.

He expected his conversation to remain private.

The Constitution protected that expectation.

The Court concluded that the government's recording device was a search.

And because the agents had not obtained a warrant, the search violated the Fourth Amendment.

The decision became known as *Katz v. United States*.

Its impact extended far beyond one phone booth.

As new technologies emerged, courts repeatedly relied on *Katz*.

Wiretaps.

Cell phones.

Computers.

GPS tracking.

Internet communications.

Again and again, judges asked the same question:

What privacy should people reasonably expect?

The Warren Court had not solved every future problem.

No court could.

But it had created a framework for protecting privacy in a changing world.

For Earl Warren, the case reflected a familiar idea.

The Constitution is not frozen in time.

Its principles must apply to new circumstances.

Otherwise, rights could disappear whenever technology changes.

The little phone booth where Charles Katz made his calls is mostly gone now.

Few remain.

But the constitutional principle born there continues to shape American law.

And another privacy case was already making its way to the Court.

This one involved marriage.

A state law.

And a deeply personal decision about whether and when a family should have children.

The case was called *Griswold v. Connecticut.*

And it would help define one of the most debated constitutional concepts of all:

The right to privacy.

Chapter 16

Privacy and the Home

By the 1960s, the Warren Court had decided cases about schools, voting, police searches, lawyers, and free speech.

Now the justices faced a different kind of question.

This one was not about a courtroom.

It was not about a voting booth.

It was not about a protest march.

It was about marriage.

And whether the government could control one of the most personal decisions a family could make.

The case began in Connecticut.

There, an old law remained on the books from the nineteenth century.

The law made it illegal for married couples to use birth control.

It even made it illegal for doctors and counselors to help married couples obtain information about it.

Many people found the law unusual.

After all, it involved decisions made between husbands and wives inside their own homes.

Still, Connecticut continued enforcing it.

One of the people who challenged the law was Estelle Griswold.

Griswold served as the Executive Director of the Planned Parenthood League of Connecticut.

She believed married couples should be free to decide whether and when to have children.

Along with Dr. C. Lee Buxton, she opened a clinic that provided information and medical advice to married couples.

The state responded quickly.

Officials arrested Griswold and Buxton.

Both were convicted.

The case eventually reached the Supreme Court.

The justices faced a difficult question.

The Constitution does not contain the word "privacy."

So where could such a right be found?

The lawyers challenging the law argued that certain personal decisions should be protected from government interference.

Marriage, they said, involves deeply private choices.

Could the government enter that space and make those choices for families?

The state argued that its law was valid.

If lawmakers had passed the law, shouldn't courts respect that decision?

The Warren Court carefully considered both sides.

The justices examined several constitutional amendments.

The First Amendment protects freedom of speech and association.

The Third protects homes from the forced quartering of soldiers.

The Fourth guards against unreasonable searches.

The Fifth protects individual rights.

Together, some justices believed, these protections created a broader zone of privacy.

Justice William O. Douglas wrote the Court's opinion.

In 1965, the Court struck down Connecticut's law.

Douglas explained that the Constitution contains "penumbras," or protections that emerge from several amendments working together.

Within those protections, he argued, exists a right to marital privacy.

The decision became known as *Griswold v. Connecticut*.

The ruling did not involve every question about privacy.

It focused specifically on married couples.

But its impact was enormous.

The Court recognized that some personal decisions belong primarily to individuals and families, not government officials.

For many Americans, the decision represented an important protection of liberty.

For others, it raised difficult questions about how courts should interpret the Constitution.

The debates would continue for decades.

Yet one thing was clear.

The Warren Court had expanded the nation's understanding of freedom.

Liberty was not only about public life.

It also involved personal choices.

Choices made inside homes.

Choices made within families.

Choices that many people believe should remain private.

As the Court continued its work, another case involving privacy and police investigations was on its way.

This one began with an unlawful arrest.

It involved evidence discovered after police broke constitutional rules.

And it would produce one of the most famous phrases in criminal law:

"The fruit of the poisonous tree."

The case was called *Wong Sun v. United States.*

And it would ask an important question:

If the government obtains evidence illegally, should it be allowed to use what it finds afterward?

Chapter 17

The Fruit of the Poisonous Tree

Imagine picking an apple from a tree.

If the tree is healthy, the fruit is healthy too.

But what if the tree is poisoned?

Would you trust the fruit growing from its branches?

That simple idea became the heart of one of the Warren Court's most important criminal procedure cases.

The case began with police officers investigating illegal drug activity.

Federal agents received information from an informant.

Following that information, officers began making arrests.

But there was a problem.

Some of those arrests were made without proper legal justification.

One of the people arrested was a man named James Wah Toy.

The officers entered his home and arrested him.

During questioning, they learned about other people who might be connected to the investigation.

One of those people was Wong Sun.

Soon, more arrests followed.

More statements were collected.

More evidence was gathered.

The government believed it had built a strong case.

But the defendants' lawyers saw something different.

They argued that the investigation had started with unconstitutional actions.

If the police violated the Constitution at the beginning, what should happen to the evidence that came later?

That question eventually reached the Supreme Court.

The Fourth Amendment protects people from unreasonable searches and seizures.

The Warren Court had already reinforced those protections in *Mapp v. Ohio*.

There, the Court ruled that illegally obtained evidence generally could not be used in state criminal trials.

Now the justices faced a new challenge.

What about evidence discovered because of an illegal arrest or search?

Should that evidence be treated differently?

The government's lawyers argued that some of the evidence was reliable.

Even if mistakes occurred earlier, they said, the later evidence should still be allowed.

The defendants disagreed.

They argued that allowing such evidence would reward unconstitutional behavior.

The Court carefully considered both positions.

The justices knew their answer would affect police investigations across the country.

In 1963, the Warren Court announced its decision.

Justice William Brennan wrote the majority opinion.

The Court ruled that evidence obtained through unconstitutional actions may be excluded if it is the product of those illegal actions.

To explain the idea, courts often use a memorable phrase:

The fruit of the poisonous tree.

If the tree—the government's original conduct—is poisoned by a constitutional violation, then the fruit that grows from it may also be tainted.

The rule does not apply in every situation.

Sometimes enough time passes.

Sometimes other lawful evidence intervenes.

Sometimes the connection becomes too weak.

But the principle remains important.

The government should not benefit from violating constitutional rights.

The decision became known as *Wong Sun v. United States.*

The case strengthened Fourth Amendment protections and helped shape modern criminal procedure.

It reminded law enforcement officers that constitutional rules matter at every stage of an investigation.

For the Warren Court, the ruling reflected a familiar theme.

Rights mean little if there is no remedy when they are violated.

The Constitution is not merely advice.

It is law.

And when government officials exceed constitutional limits, courts must sometimes act.

The decision also reinforced something the Warren Court believed deeply:

Justice requires fairness.

Not only at trial.

Not only in the courtroom.

But from the very beginning of a criminal investigation.

As the Warren Court continued its work, another case involving criminal procedure was approaching.

This one did not involve searches or arrests.

It involved a jury.

A man in Louisiana had been convicted without one.

And his challenge would help answer an important question:

When the Constitution promises a jury trial, does that promise apply in state courts too?

The case was called *Duncan v. Louisiana.*

And it would help define what fairness means when liberty is on the line.

Chapter 18

A Jury of Your Peers

In America, many people expect that if they are accused of a crime, a jury will decide their fate.

Movies show jurors listening carefully to witnesses.

Television dramas often end with a jury announcing its verdict.

The idea feels familiar.

But in the 1960s, not every criminal defendant automatically received a jury trial.

One man discovered that firsthand.

His name was Gary Duncan.

Duncan lived in Louisiana during a time of racial tension and social change.

One day, he became involved in an incident involving several teenagers.

A disagreement broke out.

Police arrested Duncan and charged him with simple battery, a misdemeanor under Louisiana law.

The charge was not considered a major felony.

But a conviction could still result in jail time.

Duncan wanted a jury trial.

He believed that ordinary citizens should help decide whether he was guilty.

The judge refused.

Under Louisiana law at the time, defendants charged with certain crimes could be tried by a judge alone.

No jury was required.

So Duncan's case proceeded without one.

The judge found him guilty.

Duncan believed something was wrong.

The Sixth Amendment guarantees the right to a speedy and public trial by an impartial jury in criminal prosecutions.

But did that right apply only in federal courts?

Or did it also apply when states prosecuted people?

That question reached the Supreme Court.

The Warren Court had already decided many cases involving the rights of criminal defendants.

It had protected the right to counsel in *Gideon*.

It had protected the right against self-incrimination in *Miranda*.

Now it faced another important question about fairness.

The justices looked closely at the history of juries.

For centuries, juries had played a central role in the justice system.

They acted as a safeguard against government abuse.

They allowed ordinary citizens to participate in the administration of justice.

And they provided another layer of protection for individual liberty.

The Court asked:

Could a state deny a jury trial when a person's freedom was at stake?

Justice Byron White wrote the majority opinion.

In 1968, the Court ruled in Duncan's favor.

The justices concluded that the right to a jury trial is fundamental to the American system of justice.

Because it is fundamental, states must generally honor it through the Fourteenth Amendment.

The decision became known as *Duncan v. Louisiana*.

The ruling did not require juries for every minor offense.

But it did require jury trials for serious criminal charges where significant penalties were possible.

The decision strengthened protections for millions of Americans.

People accused of crimes would have greater opportunities to have their cases heard by fellow citizens.

The jury system became an even more important part of state criminal courts.

For the Warren Court, the ruling reflected a familiar principle.

Government power should not operate without safeguards.

Whether through lawyers, constitutional warnings, fair searches, or juries, the justice system works best when multiple protections exist.

Each protection helps prevent mistakes.

Each protection helps preserve liberty.

And each protection reminds us that freedom can be fragile.

The Constitution protects liberty not through one right alone, but through many rights working together.

As the Warren Court continued its work, another challenge was waiting.

This one involved religion.

Students began each school day with a government-written prayer.

Many families approved.

Others objected.

The Court would have to decide whether public schools could lead students in prayer.

The case was called *Engel v. Vitale*.

And it would ask a question Americans still debate today:

What does religious freedom mean in a nation of many different beliefs?

Chapter 19

The Prayer in the Classroom

Every morning, students across America begin their school day.

They take attendance.

They greet friends.

They prepare for lessons.

But in the late 1950s, some public schools in New York began the day with something else.

A prayer.

The prayer was short.

It did not mention a specific church.

It was written by state officials and recommended for use in public schools.

The words were simple:

"Almighty God, we acknowledge our dependence upon Thee, and we beg Thy blessings upon us, our parents, our teachers and our Country."

Many people thought the prayer seemed harmless.

Students were not required to say it.

Families could choose not to participate.

Supporters believed it encouraged good values and reflected America's religious traditions.

But not everyone agreed.

Several families objected.

Some belonged to different faiths.

Others believed government should not write prayers at all.

They worried about an important constitutional principle.

The First Amendment protects religious freedom.

It guarantees that people may practice their faith.

But it also prevents the government from establishing or promoting religion.

The families asked an important question:

If government officials write a prayer and encourage students to recite it, has the government crossed a constitutional line?

The dispute eventually reached the Supreme Court.

The case became known as *Engel v. Vitale*.

The Warren Court now faced one of the most sensitive issues in American life.

Religion.

Faith is deeply important to millions of people.

Americans belong to many different religions.

Some follow Christianity.

Some practice Judaism.

Some practice Islam.

Some follow other faiths.

And some do not belong to any religion at all.

How could government respect all those beliefs equally?

The justices listened carefully.

Supporters of the prayer argued that it was voluntary and non-denominational.

No one was forced to participate.

Opponents argued that government should not be writing prayers in the first place.

Even a voluntary prayer could place pressure on students.

And government involvement in religious activities raised constitutional concerns.

The Court considered the history behind the First Amendment.

Many of the nation's founders had seen governments favor certain religions.

They wanted to protect religious liberty by keeping government from controlling religious practice.

The justices believed that protection worked both ways.

Government should not interfere with religion.

And religion should not be directed by government.

In 1962, the Court announced its decision.

Justice Hugo Black wrote the majority opinion.

The Court ruled that the state-sponsored prayer violated the Establishment Clause of the First Amendment.

Government officials could not compose official prayers for public schools.

The decision did not ban private prayer.

Students remained free to pray on their own.

People remained free to practice their faith.

Churches, synagogues, mosques, and other houses of worship remained protected.

What changed was the government's role.

The Court concluded that government should remain neutral in matters of religion.

The ruling immediately sparked controversy.

Many Americans disagreed with the decision.

Some believed the Court had gone too far.

Others believed the Court had properly protected religious freedom.

Newspapers debated the issue.

Politicians gave speeches.

Families discussed the case around dinner tables.

Even today, Americans continue to debate questions involving religion and public life.

But *Engel v. Vitale* established an important constitutional principle:

The government should not write prayers or lead religious exercises in public schools.

For the Warren Court, the case reflected a broader commitment to protecting individual liberty.

The Constitution protects people with different beliefs.

And it protects people who have no religious beliefs at all.

Religious freedom works best when government does not choose sides.

The Court's work was far from finished.

Another major case was already approaching.

This one involved prosecutors.

A criminal trial.

And evidence that had been hidden from the defense.

The Constitution promises fairness.

But what happens when important facts are kept secret?

The answer would come in *Brady v. Maryland*.

And it would reshape what prosecutors must do in the pursuit of justice.

Chapter 20

The Evidence They Didn't Share

The American justice system depends on a simple idea:

A trial should be fair.

Both sides should have a chance to present evidence.

Both sides should have a chance to challenge evidence.

And both sides should have access to important facts.

But what happens when one side knows something the other side does not?

That question brought a man named John Brady to the Supreme Court.

Brady and another man, Charles Boblit, were accused of murder in Maryland.

The crime was serious.

A person's life had been lost.

And both men faced severe consequences.

Before trial, Brady's lawyers asked prosecutors for information related to the case.

They wanted access to statements and evidence gathered during the investigation.

That request was important.

Sometimes evidence helps the prosecution.

Sometimes it helps the defense.

And sometimes it helps reveal the truth.

The prosecutors turned over some materials.

But they did not share everything.

One statement remained hidden.

In that statement, Boblit admitted that he had committed the actual killing.

The information did not necessarily prove Brady was innocent.

But it could have affected how the jury viewed his role in the crime.

The defense never saw it.

The trial went forward.

Brady was convicted.

Later, the hidden statement came to light.

When Brady learned about it, he argued that the trial had been unfair.

His lawyers believed the prosecution had a constitutional duty to disclose important evidence.

The case eventually reached the Supreme Court.

The Warren Court faced a difficult question.

Prosecutors are not ordinary lawyers.

They represent the government.

Their goal is not simply to win.

Their responsibility is to seek justice.

But what exactly does that responsibility require?

Must prosecutors share evidence that could help the accused?

Or may they decide for themselves what information to reveal?

The justices understood the importance of the issue.

Every criminal case depends on trust in the fairness of the process.

If important evidence can be hidden, how can anyone be sure justice has been done?

The Court carefully examined the facts.

The justices considered the Due Process Clause of the Fourteenth Amendment.

Due process requires fundamental fairness.

Without fairness, constitutional protections lose their meaning.

In 1963, the Court announced its decision.

Justice William O. Douglas wrote the opinion.

The Court ruled that prosecutors must disclose evidence favorable to the accused when that evidence is material to guilt or punishment.

The justices explained that justice suffers when important evidence is withheld.

The Constitution requires more than convictions.

It requires fairness.

The decision became known as *Brady v. Maryland*.

Today, lawyers often refer to favorable evidence as "Brady material."

Prosecutors across the country are required to disclose such evidence to the defense.

The rule helps reduce the risk of wrongful convictions.

It helps ensure that juries hear important facts.

And it reminds everyone involved that the search for truth matters more than winning.

For the Warren Court, the decision reflected a belief that appeared again and again throughout its cases.

The Constitution is not merely about outcomes.

It is about process.

Fair procedures protect liberty.

Fair procedures protect justice.

And fair procedures help people trust the legal system.

John Brady's case became one of the most important decisions in criminal procedure.

Its influence continues in courtrooms every day.

Whenever prosecutors review evidence.

Whenever defense lawyers request information.

Whenever judges evaluate fairness.

The legacy of *Brady v. Maryland* remains.

But another challenge was waiting.

This one involved police officers on a Cleveland street.

A detective noticed several men walking back and forth.

He became suspicious.

He stopped them.

Then he searched one of them.

The question that followed would reshape police practices across America.

The case was called *Terry v. Ohio*.

And it would ask how much suspicion is enough before police may stop and frisk someone.

Chapter 21

Stop and Frisk

One afternoon in Cleveland, Ohio, a police detective noticed something unusual.

His name was Martin McFadden.

He had spent years working as a police officer.

Experience had taught him to watch carefully.

Sometimes small details matter.

Sometimes they don't.

And sometimes they help prevent a crime.

As McFadden stood on a downtown street, he noticed three men acting strangely.

Two of them repeatedly walked past the same store window.

They would stop.

Look inside.

Walk away.

Then return again.

Over and over.

The pattern continued.

One man would look into the window.

Then another.

Then they would meet and talk.

Then start the process again.

To McFadden, it did not look like ordinary shopping.

It looked like surveillance.

He began to suspect the men were planning a robbery.

The detective decided to act.

He approached the men and identified himself as a police officer.

Then he asked questions.

The men gave answers that seemed suspicious.

McFadden remained concerned.

He worried that one or more of them might be armed.

For his own safety, he conducted a quick pat-down of their outer clothing.

When he frisked one of the men, John Terry, he discovered a handgun.

Soon Terry was arrested and charged with carrying a concealed weapon.

At trial, Terry's lawyers challenged the search.

They argued that the Fourth Amendment had been violated.

Traditionally, police needed probable cause to make an arrest.

Probable cause means there are sufficient facts to believe a crime has been committed.

But McFadden had not arrested Terry when he first stopped him.

He had only been suspicious.

Was suspicion enough?

Could police stop someone and conduct a limited search without probable cause?

The case eventually reached the Supreme Court.

The Warren Court understood that the issue affected millions of daily encounters between citizens and police officers.

The justices faced two important concerns.

First, people have constitutional rights.

The Fourth Amendment protects against unreasonable searches and seizures.

Second, police officers sometimes face dangerous situations.

They need tools to protect themselves and the public.

How could the Court balance those competing interests?

The justices listened carefully.

Terry's lawyers argued that allowing searches based on mere suspicion would give police too much power.

Without clear limits, innocent people might be stopped and searched unfairly.

The government argued that officers should not have to wait until a crime occurs before taking reasonable precautions.

A brief stop and limited pat-down could help prevent violence.

The Court worked through these concerns.

In 1968, Chief Justice Earl Warren wrote the majority opinion.

The Court ruled that police officers may briefly stop a person when they have **reasonable suspicion** that criminal activity may be occurring.

Reasonable suspicion requires more than a hunch.

An officer must be able to point to specific facts that justify the stop.

The Court also ruled that officers may conduct a limited pat-down for weapons if they reasonably believe the person may be armed and dangerous.

This type of search became known as a **Terry frisk**.

The decision became known as *Terry v. Ohio*.

Its impact was enormous.

Police departments across the country incorporated the ruling into their procedures.

Officers received training on reasonable suspicion and stop-and-frisk practices.

Courts spent decades interpreting what reasonable suspicion means.

The decision remains one of the most important Fourth Amendment cases in American history.

Yet the ruling also generated debate.

Supporters argued that it helped officers protect themselves and the public.

Critics worried that stop-and-frisk powers could be abused or applied unfairly.

Those debates continue today.

For the Warren Court, the case reflected a challenge that appeared often in constitutional law.

Liberty and security both matter.

Protecting one should not automatically destroy the other.

The Constitution often requires balancing competing values.

That work is rarely simple.

But it is necessary.

The Warren Court was nearing the end of its remarkable era.

Yet one final challenge remained.

The criticism had grown louder.

Across parts of America, angry signs appeared.

Billboards carried a message aimed directly at the Chief Justice.

The words were impossible to miss:

"Impeach Earl Warren."

The next chapter would explore why so many people opposed the Warren Court—and why Earl Warren refused to back down.

Chapter 22

Impeach Earl Warren!

By the late 1960s, Earl Warren had become one of the most famous—and controversial—people in America.

The Warren Court had changed public schools.

It had expanded voting rights.

It had strengthened protections for criminal defendants.

It had defended free speech.

It had protected freedom of the press.

It had struck down laws banning interracial marriage.

Many Americans celebrated these decisions.

Many others did not.

Some believed the Court had gone too far.

Others believed it was moving too fast.

Still others argued that judges should not make decisions that changed long-standing traditions.

As the criticism grew louder, a movement began.

Across parts of the country, giant billboards appeared.

Some stood beside highways.

Others appeared near towns and cities.

The message was simple and direct:

"Impeach Earl Warren."

The signs shocked many Americans.

Impeachment is a serious process used to remove government officials from office.

The people behind the campaign wanted Warren removed as Chief Justice.

One of the movement's most visible leaders was Robert Welch, founder of the John Birch Society.

The organization strongly opposed many Warren Court decisions.

Its members believed the Court was changing America in dangerous ways.

To them, Warren represented everything they disliked about the Court's direction.

But the criticism did not stop with billboards.

Letters poured into Washington.

Newspapers published angry editorials.

Radio commentators criticized Court decisions.

Politicians gave speeches attacking the justices.

Sometimes the criticism became personal.

People questioned Warren's motives.

They questioned his judgment.

They questioned his leadership.

For many people, the pressure would have been overwhelming.

But Earl Warren had experienced controversy before.

He understood that important decisions rarely please everyone.

The Constitution often requires courts to protect rights even when those rights are unpopular.

That can make judges targets of criticism.

Warren accepted that reality.

He believed the Court's responsibility was not to follow public opinion.

Its responsibility was to follow the Constitution.

The criticism hurt.

But it did not change his commitment.

He continued leading the Court.

He continued listening to arguments.

He continued writing opinions.

And he continued working with the other justices to decide difficult cases.

Inside the Supreme Court building, life went on.

Cases continued arriving.

Lawyers continued arguing.

The Constitution continued raising new questions.

The justices knew that public criticism was part of their job.

Sometimes people praised them.

Sometimes people protested them.

The Court could not control either response.

What it could control was the quality of its work.

History would eventually judge the Warren Court.

And history's judgment has been significant.

Today, many of the Warren Court's most controversial decisions are considered landmarks of American law.

Students study them.

Lawyers cite them.

Judges rely on them.

Citizens benefit from them.

But at the time, none of that was guaranteed.

The future was uncertain.

Earl Warren knew that.

He also knew something else.

The Constitution belongs to every generation.

Each generation must decide whether to live up to its promises.

Courts can interpret those promises.

Judges can defend them.

But judges cannot protect liberty alone.

That responsibility belongs to the people too.

The campaign to impeach Warren never succeeded.

He remained Chief Justice until 1969.

Yet the controversy revealed something important about American democracy.

People are free to disagree.

They are free to criticize public officials.

They are free to challenge decisions.

Even Supreme Court decisions.

In many ways, those freedoms existed because of the very Constitution Warren and his colleagues worked to protect.

As his years on the Court drew to a close, Warren began reflecting on what had been accomplished.

The Court had changed schools, elections, criminal justice, free speech, privacy, and civil rights.

But Warren knew the story was larger than any one justice.

Larger than any one Court.

Larger than any one generation.

And in his final years, he began thinking about the future.

The next chapter is about that reflection.

It is about the legacy of the Warren Court.

And about a challenge that now belongs to all of us.

Chapter 23

A Republic, If You Can Keep It

In 1969, Earl Warren stepped down as Chief Justice of the United States.

For sixteen years, he had sat in the center chair.

For sixteen years, he had worked alongside some of the most influential justices in American history.

Together, they had decided cases that changed the nation.

The work had not always been easy.

Some people praised the Court.

Others criticized it.

Some celebrated its decisions.

Others protested them.

Yet through it all, the Warren Court had asked the same question again and again:

What does the Constitution require?

The answers reshaped American life.

Children could no longer be separated in public schools because of race.

Poor defendants gained the right to a lawyer.

Police officers had to respect constitutional limits.

Students retained free speech rights.

Newspapers received greater protection when criticizing public officials.

Married couples gained greater privacy.

Votes became more equal.

Native nations strengthened their sovereignty.

Interracial marriage became protected throughout the nation.

These changes did not happen overnight.

And they did not happen because of one person alone.

Earl Warren often received the attention.

After all, his name was attached to the Court.

But the Warren Court was a team.

Justices Hugo Black, William Brennan, William O. Douglas, John Marshall Harlan, Tom Clark, Potter Stewart, Byron White, Arthur Goldberg, Abe Fortas, and many others helped shape its decisions.

And one of the most remarkable journeys belonged to Thurgood Marshall.

Years earlier, Marshall had stood before the Court arguing *Brown v. Board of Education*.

He had challenged segregation as a lawyer.

Then, in 1967, he joined the Supreme Court itself.

The lawyer who helped persuade the Court became one of the justices helping decide future cases.

It was a powerful reminder that history keeps moving.

As Warren reflected on his years of service, he understood something important.

The Constitution is not self-executing.

Its promises do not become real simply because they are written on paper.

Words matter.

But actions matter too.

The Constitution depends on people.

Judges.

Lawyers.

Teachers.

Students.

Voters.

Parents.

Citizens.

Each generation inherits the promises of the Constitution.

And each generation decides what to do with them.

That responsibility did not end when Earl Warren retired.

It did not end when the Warren Court changed.

And it does not end today.

Long before Warren's time, another famous American had been asked what kind of government the Constitutional Convention had created.

Benjamin Franklin reportedly answered:

"A republic, if you can keep it."

Those words remained relevant during Warren's years.

They remain relevant now.

A republic is more than elections.

More than courts.

More than laws.

A republic depends on citizens who understand their rights and responsibilities.

It depends on people willing to listen, learn, participate, and care.

The Warren Court helped define many constitutional freedoms.

But no court can preserve those freedoms alone.

Judges can interpret the Constitution.

Courts can issue decisions.

But citizens must decide whether those principles will live in everyday life.

Will people treat one another fairly?

Will they respect the rights of those with whom they disagree?

Will they protect liberty for everyone, not just themselves?

Those questions belong to every generation.

Including yours.

The story of Earl Warren is not really about one man.

It is about a nation struggling to live up to its ideals.

It is about ordinary people who brought extraordinary cases.

Linda Brown.

Clarence Gideon.

Ernesto Miranda.

Charles Katz.

Richard and Mildred Loving.

Mary Beth Tinker.
Dollree Mapp.
Gary Duncan.
And many others.
They were not famous when their journeys began.
They were students.
Parents.
Workers.
Prisoners.
Neighbors.
Citizens.
Yet their stories changed the Constitution.
And through those changes, they changed America.
That is the legacy of the Warren Court.
Not simply the opinions written.
Not simply the cases decided.
But the people whose lives gave those cases meaning.
The story ends where every constitutional story eventually ends:
With us.

The Constitution's future is not hidden in a courtroom. It is not locked inside a law book.

It lives wherever people choose to make its promises real.
The Warren Court helped light the way.
Now the path belongs to the next generation.
A republic, if we can keep it.

Chapter 24

The Super Chief

Years after Earl Warren left the Supreme Court, people still talked about him.

Some remembered the criticism.

Some remembered the protests.

Some remembered the billboards demanding his removal.

But many remembered something else.

They remembered the leadership.

Among the justices who served with him, Earl Warren earned a nickname:

The Super Chief.

It was not an official title.

It was not written into law.

And it did not come from a newspaper headline.

It came from the people who worked beside him.

The nickname reflected Warren's unusual ability to bring people together.

The Supreme Court is not a place where everyone agrees.

Nine justices often arrive with different backgrounds, different experiences, and different ideas about the Constitution.

Strong disagreements are common.

Yet Warren had a gift.

He listened.

He persuaded.

He built consensus.

He believed that when possible, the Court should speak with one voice.

That belief helped produce one of the most important decisions in American history.

When the Court considered *Brown v. Board of Education*, some feared the justices might divide.

A split decision could weaken the ruling.

Warren worked patiently with his colleagues.

He encouraged discussion.

He built trust.

And eventually, every justice joined the opinion.

The result was unanimous.

The nation heard a single message:

Separate schools are inherently unequal.

That moment became one of the defining achievements of the Warren Court.

But Warren's leadership extended far beyond *Brown*.

Throughout sixteen years as Chief Justice, he guided the Court through questions involving civil rights, criminal justice, voting, free speech, privacy, religion, and equality.

The Court did not always agree.

No court ever does.

Yet Warren helped create an environment where difficult conversations could happen.

That may be one reason his colleagues respected him so deeply.

Leadership is not only about making decisions.

Sometimes it is about helping others work together.

The Warren Court also reminds us that history is made by teams.

People often focus on one famous figure.

But every landmark decision involved many voices.

Hugo Black.

William Brennan.

William O. Douglas.

John Marshall Harlan.

Potter Stewart.

Tom Clark.

Byron White.

Arthur Goldberg.

Abe Fortas.

Thurgood Marshall.

And others who served during those sixteen years.
Each justice brought something important to the Court.
Some agreed with Warren often.
Some disagreed.
Yet together they shaped constitutional law for generations.
And then there were the people outside the Court.
The litigants.
The ordinary citizens.
The people whose names became case names.
Linda Brown.
Clarence Gideon.
Dollree Mapp.
Ernesto Miranda.
Mary Beth Tinker.
Charles Katz.
Gary Duncan.
Richard and Mildred Loving.
Paul and Marena Williams.
John Brady.
John Terry.
L. B. Sullivan.
And many others.
Without them, there would have been no Warren Court legacy.
The Constitution comes alive through people.
Real people.
People with families, jobs, worries, hopes, and dreams.
People who encounter a problem and decide to speak up.
Sometimes they win.
Sometimes they lose.
But their stories help define what constitutional rights mean.
That is why the Warren Court remains so important.
Its legacy is not simply a collection of cases.

It is a collection of human stories.

Stories about equality.

Stories about liberty.

Stories about fairness.

Stories about belonging.

As the years passed, many of the Court's decisions became woven into everyday American life.

Students expect free speech rights.

Defendants expect lawyers.

Citizens expect equal voting power.

Families expect privacy.

Journalists expect freedom to criticize public officials.

These expectations did not appear by accident.

They grew from constitutional struggles fought by ordinary people.

And that brings us back to the question Earl Warren left behind.

What happens next?

The answer is not found in the past.

It is found in the future.

It is found in classrooms.

In communities.

In voting booths.

In courtrooms.

In conversations.

And in the choices made by each new generation.

The Warren Court helped write an important chapter in America's constitutional story.

But the story itself is still being written.

The next chapter belongs to you.

Chapter 25

The Constitution Lives Through You

We the People

Article 1

Imagine walking through a museum filled with American history.

You see photographs of the Little Rock Nine.

A copy of the Constitution.

A black armband like the ones worn by Mary Beth Tinker and her classmates.

A newspaper carrying the story of *Brown v. Board of Education*.

A picture of Richard and Mildred Loving.

A handwritten petition from Clarence Gideon.

A sign that reads: "Impeach Earl Warren!"

At first, these objects might seem unrelated.

But they are all connected by a single idea.

The Constitution.

Not the paper itself.

Not the ink.

The promise.

Throughout this book, ordinary people stepped into extraordinary moments.

Linda Brown wanted to attend a neighborhood school.

Clarence Gideon wanted a lawyer.

Ernesto Miranda wanted fair treatment.

Mary Beth Tinker wanted to express her opinion.

Richard and Mildred Loving wanted to live together as husband and wife.

Charles Katz wanted privacy.

Gary Duncan wanted a jury.

Each person brought a question to the courts.

And each question helped America decide what freedom means.

That is one of the most remarkable things about constitutional law.

It is not only made by presidents, senators, or judges.

It is also shaped by students.

Parents.

Workers.

Journalists.

Neighbors.

Citizens.

People just like you.

When Earl Warren became Chief Justice in 1953, he inherited a Constitution that was nearly two centuries old.

Yet the questions facing the nation were brand new.

How should constitutional rights apply in modern schools?

How should they apply to telephones?

To voting districts?

To police investigations?

To racial equality?

The Warren Court did not answer every question.

No court ever can.

New challenges appear with every generation.

Today's questions may involve the internet.

Artificial intelligence.

Social media.

New forms of communication.

New technologies.

New ideas about freedom and equality.

The Constitution remains the same document.

But each generation must decide how its principles apply to new circumstances.

That is why constitutional law is never truly finished.

The story continues.

Perhaps one day you will become a lawyer.

Or a judge.

Or a teacher.

Or a journalist.

Perhaps you will run for office.

Or organize your community.

Or simply vote and participate in civic life.

Whatever path you choose, the Constitution belongs to you.

Its promises belong to you.

Its responsibilities belong to you as well.

Earl Warren understood that.

Near the end of his life, he reflected on the work of the Court.

He knew that judges alone could not create justice.

They could interpret the law.

They could protect rights.

But they could not make people care about freedom.

That responsibility belongs to citizens.

It belongs to all of us.

The Warren Court helped expand the meaning of equality, liberty, fairness, and dignity.

But preserving those ideals is an ongoing task.

Each generation receives the Constitution as an inheritance.

Each generation leaves it behind for the next.

The question is always the same:

Will we leave it stronger?

That is why the story of the Warren Court matters.

Not because it happened long ago.

Not because it appears in textbooks.

Not because students study the cases.

It matters because the questions those people asked are still with us.

Who belongs?

What is fair?

How should power be limited?

What does freedom require?

And how can a nation live up to its promises?

Those questions do not belong to Earl Warren anymore.

They belong to us.

And someday, they will belong to those who come after us. The Constitution lives only when people bring it to life.

The next chapter of that story has not been written yet. Perhaps you will help write it.

Chapter 26

Meet the Warren Court

By now, you've met many of the people whose cases changed America.

Linda Brown.

Clarence Gideon.

Mary Beth Tinker.

Richard and Mildred Loving.

And many others.

But who were the people making these decisions?

Who sat on the Supreme Court during the Warren years?

The answer changed over time.

Justices retired.

New justices joined.

Presidents made appointments.

Yet throughout Earl Warren's sixteen years as Chief Justice, a remarkable group of men helped shape constitutional law.

One of the most influential was **Justice William Brennan**.

Brennan was known for building agreement among the justices.

He often helped write opinions that expanded individual rights.

Many historians consider him one of the most important justices in Supreme Court history.

Then there was **Justice Hugo Black**.

Before joining the Court, Black had served in the United States Senate.

On the Court, he became a strong defender of constitutional freedoms, especially free speech and the protections found in the Bill of Rights.

Justice William O. Douglas served longer than any justice in American history.

Douglas believed deeply in personal liberty and often argued that constitutional rights should be interpreted broadly to protect individual freedom.

Justice John Marshall Harlan II frequently challenged the majority.

He did not always agree with Warren or Brennan.

Yet his thoughtful opinions earned widespread respect.

Many of his dissents later influenced future courts.

Justice Tom Clark, a former Attorney General of the United States, brought experience from law enforcement and public service.

He helped shape many important decisions during the Warren era.

Justice Potter Stewart often occupied the middle ground.

He carefully considered each case and frequently played an important role in closely divided decisions.

Justice Byron White, a former football star and Rhodes Scholar, joined the Court in 1962.

He would continue serving long after Warren retired.

Justice Arthur Goldberg served only a few years on the Court, but he participated in several landmark decisions, including cases involving privacy and individual rights.

Later, **Justice Abe Fortas** joined the Court.

Before becoming a justice, he had argued Clarence Gideon's case before the Supreme Court.

His journey from advocate to justice reflected the close connection between law and constitutional change.

And then there was **Justice Thurgood Marshall**.

Marshall's story was unique.

Years before joining the Court, he argued *Brown v. Board of Education*.

He traveled across the country fighting segregation and discrimination.

In 1967, he became the first Black justice in Supreme Court history.

The lawyer who had persuaded the Court in *Brown* now sat on the bench helping decide future constitutional questions.

Together, these justices did not always agree.

Sometimes they argued fiercely.

Sometimes they wrote separate opinions.

Sometimes they dissented.

But that is part of how the Supreme Court works.

The justices examine different sides of difficult questions.

They challenge one another's ideas.

They search for answers in the Constitution.

The Warren Court became famous not because everyone thought alike.

It became famous because it confronted some of the nation's hardest problems.

And through those cases, the justices helped shape the rights and freedoms Americans experience today.

Chief Justice Earl Warren may have sat in the center chair.

But history was written by an entire Court.

A team of justices.

A nation of citizens.

And ordinary people brave enough to bring extraordinary cases.

Chapter 27

The Cases That Still Live Today

When Earl Warren retired in 1969, the work of the Supreme Court did not stop.

New justices took their seats.

New cases arrived.

New generations faced new challenges.

Yet many of the Warren Court's decisions continued shaping American life.

In fact, you probably encounter their influence more often than you realize.

Think about school.

Students today can express opinions in ways that would have been difficult before *Tinker v. Des Moines*.

They may write for student newspapers.

Join clubs.

Speak at meetings.

Or peacefully express their beliefs.

The rules are not unlimited, but the Constitution still follows them through the schoolhouse gate.

Think about voting.

Because of *Baker v. Carr* and *Reynolds v. Sims*, states must pay attention to population when drawing legislative districts.

The idea that every vote should carry roughly equal weight remains a cornerstone of American democracy.

Think about police and criminal courts.

If someone cannot afford a lawyer, *Gideon v. Wainwright* still matters.

If police question a suspect in custody, *Miranda v. Arizona* still matters.

If prosecutors discover evidence that could help the defense, *Brady v. Maryland* still matters.

If police conduct an unlawful search, *Mapp v. Ohio* and *Wong Sun v. United States* still matter.

These cases continue influencing thousands of courtrooms every day.

Think about freedom of speech.

Newspapers, reporters, and citizens still rely on *New York Times v. Sullivan* when criticizing public officials.

The case remains one of the strongest protections for free public debate in American history.

Think about privacy.

The world today includes smartphones, laptops, social media, and technologies the Warren Court could never have imagined.

Yet courts still look back to *Katz v. United States* and *Griswold v. Connecticut* when asking how privacy should work in a modern world.

Think about equality.

The promise of *Brown v. Board of Education* continues to inspire people seeking equal opportunity.

The promise of *Loving v. Virginia* continues to remind Americans that the law should not divide people based on race.

And think about sovereignty.

Native nations continue to rely on principles reinforced by *Williams v. Lee* as they exercise authority over their communities and courts.

These cases are not dusty relics locked away in law books.

They are living parts of American life.

Every generation returns to them.

Sometimes courts follow them closely.

Sometimes courts reinterpret them.

Sometimes courts debate their meaning.

That is how constitutional law works.

The Constitution remains the same document.

But people continue discussing what its promises require.

Some Warren Court decisions remain popular.

Others remain controversial.

Reasonable people still disagree about many of them.

That is part of democracy too.

The Constitution protects the freedom to debate constitutional meaning.

What matters is that citizens continue engaging with those questions.

Because constitutional rights survive only when people understand them.

That may be the Warren Court's most important lesson.

The Constitution belongs to everyone.

Not just judges.

Not just lawyers.

Not just government officials.

Everyone.

And when ordinary people learn their rights, exercise their rights, and defend the rights of others, the Constitution becomes more than words on paper.

It becomes part of everyday life.

That was true for Linda Brown.

It was true for Clarence Gideon.

It was true for Mary Beth Tinker.

And it can be true for you.

The Warren Court's story may have begun in the 1950s.

But its influence continues today.

And tomorrow.
And in every generation that follows.

Chapter 28

Keep the Republic

One afternoon in 1787, as the delegates left the Constitutional Convention in Philadelphia, a woman stopped Benjamin Franklin.

She had watched the delegates come and go for months.

Now the Constitution was finished.

She asked Franklin a simple question.

"What have you given us?"

Franklin answered,

"A republic, if you can keep it."

More than 175 years later, Earl Warren understood exactly what Franklin meant.

The Constitution is not magic.

It does not protect itself.

The words on its pages matter only if people are willing to defend them.

During the Warren Court years, ordinary Americans tested those promises.

A little girl wanted to attend her neighborhood school.

A prisoner wanted a lawyer.

A married couple wanted to live together.

Students wanted to wear black armbands.

A newspaper wanted to report the truth.

A Navajo family wanted their own court to decide their case.

A man wanted privacy in a phone booth.

A voter wanted an equal voice.

None of them knew they would become part of history.

They simply believed the Constitution should mean what it says.

The Warren Court listened.

Sometimes it agreed.

Sometimes it drew new constitutional lines.

Sometimes it reminded America that rights written on paper must also exist in real life.

But the story did not end there.

Every generation inherits new questions.

Should new technology change our privacy?

How should free speech work online?

How do we protect voting rights?

How do we balance safety and liberty?

What does equality require today?

The answers will not come from Earl Warren.

Or William Brennan.

Or Thurgood Marshall.

Or Hugo Black.

Their work is finished.

Now the responsibility belongs to us.

Perhaps one day you will become a lawyer.

Perhaps you will become a teacher.

A journalist.

A police officer.

A judge.

A legislator.

Or perhaps you will simply become an informed citizen who votes, asks questions, and stands up for what is right.

Every one of those roles matters.

Because democracy is not something spectators watch.

It is something citizens build.

Earl Warren often said that the Constitution must serve real people.

Not just governments.

Not just institutions.

People.

The children in classrooms.

The families in their homes.

The voters at the polls.

The defendants in courtrooms.

The reporters asking difficult questions.

The citizens whose voices deserve to be heard.

That is the story of the Warren Court.

Not simply a collection of famous cases.

But a reminder that justice grows when ordinary people have the courage to ask extraordinary questions.

And so this story ends where America's constitutional story always begins—

With you.

Will you learn your rights?

Will you respect the rights of others?

Will you help make your community more fair, more just, and more equal?

Those choices belong to every generation. Benjamin Franklin left us with a challenge. Earl Warren spent sixteen years trying to answer it. Now it is your turn.

A republic, if you can keep it.

Appendix A

Warren Court Timeline (1953–1969)

The Warren Court decided hundreds of cases, but the ones in this book helped shape the rights Americans enjoy today.

Year	*Case*	*What Changed?*
1954	**Brown v. Board of Education**	Segregated public schools were declared unconstitutional.
1959	**Williams v. Lee**	Tribal courts retained authority over many disputes on reservation land.
1961	**Mapp v. Ohio**	Evidence obtained through unconstitutional searches generally cannot be used in court.
1962	**Baker v. Carr**	Federal courts may hear challenges to unfair voting districts.
1962	**Engel v. Vitale**	Government-written school prayers violate the First Amendment.
1963	**Gideon v. Wainwright**	People charged with serious crimes who cannot afford lawyers must be provided one.
1963	**Brady v. Maryland**	Prosecutors must disclose important evidence favorable to the accused.
1963	**Wong Sun v. United States**	Evidence resulting from unconstitutional police conduct may be excluded from trial.
1964	**New York Times v. Sullivan**	Public officials must prove "actual malice" to win most defamation lawsuits.
1964	**Reynolds v. Sims**	State legislative districts must provide equal representation: "one person, one vote."
1965	**Griswold v. Connecticut**	Married couples have a constitutional right to marital privacy.
1966	**Miranda v. Arizona**	Police must inform suspects of important constitutional rights before custodial questioning.
1967	**Katz v. United States**	The Fourth Amendment protects people, not just places.

1967	**United States v. Wade**	Defendants have the right to a lawyer at post-indictment lineups.
1967	**Loving v. Virginia**	States cannot ban interracial marriage.
1968	**Duncan v. Louisiana**	States must provide jury trials for serious criminal offenses.
1968	**Terry v. Ohio**	Police may briefly stop and frisk someone based on reasonable suspicion.
1969	**Tinker v. Des Moines**	Students keep their constitutional free speech rights in school.

The Warren Court at a Glance

Chief Justice

- **Earl Warren** (1953–1969)

Associate Justices who served during the Warren Court

- Hugo Black
- William O. Douglas
- Felix Frankfurter
- John Marshall Harlan II
- Tom C. Clark
- William J. Brennan, Jr.
- Charles E. Whittaker
- Potter Stewart
- Byron White
- Arthur Goldberg
- Abe Fortas
- Thurgood Marshall

Why These Cases Matter

The Warren Court reminded America that the Constitution belongs to everyone.

Not only presidents.

Not only judges.

Not only lawyers.

But students.

Parents.

Journalists.

Police officers.

Teachers.

Voters.

Families.

And children who simply ask, "Is this fair?"

The Constitution continues to grow through the courage of ordinary people willing to stand up for their rights. That is the enduring legacy of the Warren Court. **A republic, if you can keep it.**

Also by Joseline Hardrick

Love Law Legacy Lawyers Who Were Florida's Firsts
None But Ourselves A Journey Through Self-Liberation
Justice & Liberty for All - A Chapter Book About Supreme Court Cases That Changed America
All Rise A Day at the Courthouse
Chief Justice Earl Warren and the People Behind the Constitutional Revolution A Chapter Book

Watch for more at https://lawyerish.org.

About the Author

Empowering Every Legal Journey™

At Lawyerish® we empower the next generation of legal professionals.

We are dedicated to providing resources, insights, and inspiration for those who are law-adjacent and anyone aspiring to make a positive impact in the legal field.

Read more at https://thelawyerish.com/.